CHACO CULTURE NATIONAL PARK

A TRUE BOOK

by
David Petersen

Children's Press®
A Division of Grolier Publishing
New York London Hong Kong Sydney
Danbury, Connecticut

Subject Consultant
Russ Bodner
Interpretive Specialist
Chaco Culture National Park

Reading Consultant
Linda Cornwell
Coordinator of School Quality
and Professional Improvement
Indiana State Teachers
Association

This girl's beads and headdress celebrate Anasazi culture.

Visit Children's Press® on the
Internet at:
http://publishing.grolier.com

Library of Congress Cataloging-in-Publication Data

Petersen, David, 1946—
    Chaco Culture National Historical Park / by David Petersen.
        p.   cm. — (A true book)
    Includes bibliographical references and index.
    Summary: Describes the history, landscape, wildlife, and activities
available for visitors at Chaco Culture National Historical Park in New
Mexico.
    ISBN: 0-516-20942-6   (lib.bdg.)   0-516-26757-4 (pbk.)
    1. Chaco Culture National Historic Park (N.M.)—Juvenile literature.
[1. Chaco Culture National Historic Park (N.M.) 2. National parks and
reserves. 3. Pueblo Indians—New Mexico 4. Indians of North
America—New Mexico] I. Title. II. Series.
F802.C4P48 1999
978.9'82—dc21   98-42467
                                                              CIP
                                                              AC

GROLIER
PUBLISHING   1 2 3 4 5 6 7 8 9 10 R 08 07 06 05 04 03 02 01 00 99

Contents

UTAH COLORADO KANSAS

ARIZONA NEW MEXICO OKLAHOMA

TEXAS

CHACO CULTURE NATIONAL HISTORIC PARK

COLORADO

Santa Fe

ARIZONA

NEW MEXICO

Rio Grande

TEXAS

CHACO CULTURE NATIONAL HISTORIC PARK

Chaco Wash

Kin Kletso

Pueblo Bonito

Chetro Ketl

Pueblo del Arroyo

CHACO CANYON

Casa Rinconada

Visitor Center

0   4 miles

0   6 kilometers

Chaco Canyon

Way out in New Mexico, in the heart of the American West, there is a haunted canyon. The spirits who live there are as real as rock. You can't see them, of course. But you can hear their breezy whispers in the leaves of cottonwood trees. You can feel their gentle presence as you wander among the towering ruins of the houses they built and occupied—a thousand years ago.

Chaco is the canyon's name. It's an ancient name, possibly Navajo, whose meaning has been lost. Twisting like a thin green snake down the canyon's broad, flat belly is cottonwood-shaded Chaco Wash. Sometimes it carries water. More often it does not.

Chaco Wash sometimes fills with water that flows past thirsty cottonwood trees.

Chaco Canyon is about 16 miles (26 kilometers) long, 1.5 miles (2.4 km) wide, and 300 feet (91 meters) deep. Its north wall is a vertical cliff. The south wall rises more gently. The people who built the great stone structures of Chaco were not the first to visit the canyon. For 10,000 years, human voices have echoed from its walls. The earliest visitors were wandering hunters and gatherers, just passing through.

The remains of this structure stand near the canyon's north wall.

Then, about A.D. 400, a people we call the Anasazi arrived at Chaco. Anasazi is a Navajo word that means "the ancient ones." But the Anasazi were not related to

This woman's turquoise necklace is a reminder of her Anasazi ancestors.

the Navajo. Rather, they were ancestors of today's Pueblo Indians of Arizona and New Mexico. The Anasazi came to farm and to build beautiful stone cities at Chaco Canyon and elsewhere throughout the American Southwest.

They handcrafted delicate painted pottery, carved and painted wooden flutes, and crafted jewelry from turquoise —a semiprecious stone, blue-green as a desert sky.

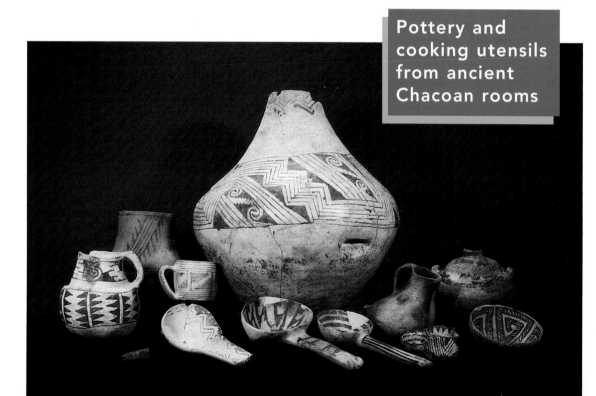

Pottery and cooking utensils from ancient Chacoan rooms

Among the thousands of Anasazi artifacts unearthed at Chaco are bracelets and neck-laces containing thousands of beads . . . a life-size frog of polished jet (hard coal), with bulging turquoise eyes and a turquoise-studded collar . . . copper bells, plus parrot and

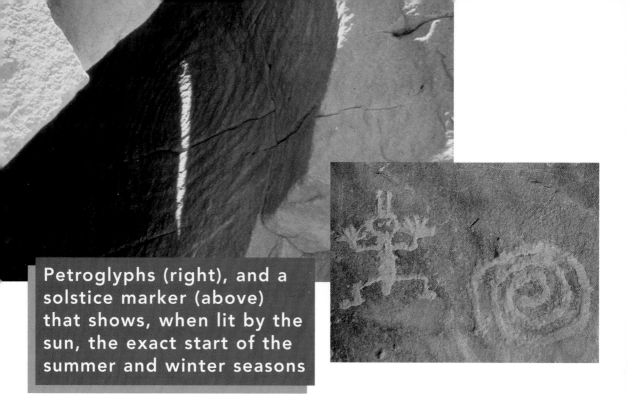

Petroglyphs (right), and a solstice marker (above) that shows, when lit by the sun, the exact start of the summer and winter seasons

macaw feathers from Mexico . . . and "trumpets" made from seashells.

Chaco Canyon also contains many rock paintings, called pictographs, and rock etchings, called petroglyphs.

Architecture— A Chacoan Art

The Chaco people's highest art form was the great stone structures they built.

Today, Chaco Canyon is world famous for its giant prehistoric buildings, which resemble apartments and are called Great Houses. Each of

A view of the Kin Kletso ruin

Chaco's many Great Houses stood several stories high and contained hundreds of rooms. Only four of these Great Houses have been excavated.

The Great Houses were large enough to house hundreds or even thousands of people. But researchers believe that only a few important people occupied them full-time. Chaco Canyon, it is believed, was a center for trade and religious ceremony. The Great Houses may have served as hotels for the many visitors, as churches or government buildings, or all three.

Such large, lovely, and lasting structures as Chaco's Great

Main Street, Chaco Canyon, as it may have once looked

Houses required a miracle of engineering and labor. Ancient builders cut and carried thousands of stone slabs from nearby cliffs and hundreds of huge logs from distant mountain forests. Anasazi construction tools were made of stone, bone, and wood. A single large building could have taken centuries to build.

After sandstone slabs were collected and carried to a building site, they were squared to make building blocks. The blocks were carefully stacked to make strong, graceful walls. To cement the stone walls together, the workers used mud mortar. When

Examples of Chacoan masonry (above) and carpentry (right)

finished, the walls were plastered with more mud.

In addition to hundreds of living and storage rooms, each Great House had several cellar-like chambers called kivas.

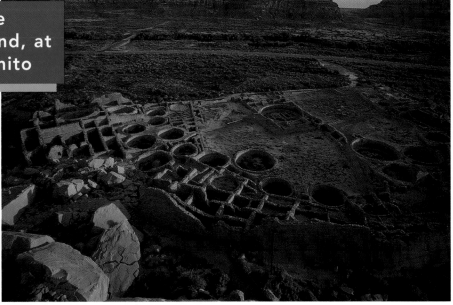

Large, stone-paved plazas provided space for work, play, and ceremony.

Clustered around Chaco's Great Houses, like moons orbiting planets, were hundreds of small farming villages, called pueblos.

To make climbing in and out of their canyon city easier and safer, the Chaco residents carved huge stairways into the steep sandstone cliffs and built great earthen ramps.

Two hikers descend a stony staircase in the Kin Kletso ruin.

Why Chaco?

One likely reason the
Anasazi chose to build their
cultural center at Chaco was
the canyon's central location
in their world. Beautiful
mountains, rivers, and mesas
(high, flat areas) surround
Chaco. These remain sacred
to local Indians even today,

The dry land, though beautiful, was a challenge to farm.

as surely they were for the Anasazi centuries ago.

In spite of its beauty, the sandy soil would have been difficult to farm, and water has always been scarce there. But by constructing dams, ponds, and irrigation ditches, the ancient engineers were able to channel what water they had to their gardens of beans, corn, and squash.

To connect Chaco with the outside world, roads fanned

out in every direction, like spokes from the hub of a wheel. Some of the ancient roadways are still visible today. Following these roads to Chaco came visitors from as far away as Mexico.

It is likely that Chaco was not just a center for trade, but a shrine, or holy city, as well.

The largest structure at Chaco is Pueblo Bonito— Spanish for "Pretty Village." Shaped like a giant letter D,

Pueblo Bonito stood at least four stories high, with thirty-seven kivas, six hundred to eight hundred rooms, and two spacious plazas.

Next largest is Chetro Ketl, called the Rain Pueblo, a Great House of five hundred rooms stacked four stories high, with sixteen kivas and a large plaza.

The great kiva at Chetro Ketl

Kiva, Kiva, Kiva

What, exactly, is a kiva?

Kivas are below the ground ceremonial chambers, usually round in shape, and quite small. Stone benches ring the walls. An open fire provided light and heat. The smoke escaped through a hole in the flat roof. This same hole, with a ladder, was used to enter and exit the kiva. Kivas provided family groups, or clans, with private, protected places to gather, work, and worship.

Not all kivas were small and private. Some were huge public places, like ancient underground cathedrals.

Like Pueblo Bonito, Chetro Ketl is D-shaped, and built close against the canyon's north wall.

Among the smaller Chacoan Great Houses is Pueblo del Arroyo—in Spanish "Village by the Wash"—with 280 rooms and twenty kivas.

Ruins at Pueblo del Arroyo

A dusting of snow fills the largest known kiva at Casa Rinconada.

The largest excavated kiva at Chaco is Casa Rinconada— Spanish for "House in the Corner." Its sunken bowl measures 63.5 feet (19 m) across, with a roof 12 feet (3.6 m) high. Two stone stairways descend into the spacious chamber.

Since Casa Rinconada is aligned with the North Star, it may have been used to mark and celebrate the beginning of summer—an important event for a farming people.

And these are just a few of the hundreds of prehistoric wonders awaiting you at Chaco!

And Then They Were Gone...

Why, after building their greatest city there, did the Anasazi leave Chaco Canyon?

For centuries the Anasazi had made their living from the land. They farmed, logged, hunted, gathered wild plants, and built great cities—not only at Chaco, but at Salmon Ruins and Aztec Ruins in northern New Mexico, at Mesa Verde (now a national park) in southwestern Colorado, and many other locations. As their population grew ever larger, the natural resources upon which they depended became ever scarcer.

Then, about A.D. 1130, a fifty-year drought began. With no water for their crops,

Rain clouds gather over the canyon floor.

and with trees, wildlife, and other natural resources running out, the Ancient Ones were forced to abandon their holy city. They fanned out and relocated to other, more habitable areas throughout the Southwest.

By A.D. 1150, three centuries after its founding, Chaco was a ghost town. Yet, even today, you can sense gentle Anasazi spirits haunting the magnificent ruins of this great canyon city.

Visiting Chaco— A Wild West Adventure

Chaco Canyon remains hidden from the modern world. The park entrance roads are long, unpaved, and can be muddy and snow packed. There are no motels or restaurants in the park, and only one campground. And the nearest

CHACO CULTURE
NATIONAL
HISTORICAL PARK
20 MILES

CHACO CULTURE
CAMPGROUND
USUALLY

Full By Noon
April - October

Read the road sign carefully, and come prepared to rough it!

small town is 71 miles (114 km) away.

But for those who meet the challenge and come—and people come from the world over—Chaco Canyon is a Wild West adventure.

At the park visitor's center
you'll find maps, photos, videos,
modern restrooms, and drinking
water. There's a museum containing Chacoan artifacts, and

friendly rangers to answer all your questions—including how to become a Chaco Junior Ranger.

Chaco is a walking park. And along its miles of trails, you can expect to meet some of the canyon's wilder residents. Big collared lizards and smaller side-blotched lizards are common everywhere. And gopher snakes—big, lazy, and harmless—are often seen near the ruins.

A collared lizard (above) and a gopher snake (right)

Chaco also has rattlesnakes. If you see one, or hear its grasshopperlike warning buzz, stay back and leave it alone. The frightened reptile will return the favor.

Owls (above) and coyotes (right) add their special sounds to the desert night.

Common Chaco mammals include rabbits, prairie dogs, coyotes, badgers, and many others. At night, listen for the chirping of bats, the yelping of coyotes, and the eerie hooting of owls.

In 1907, Chaco Canyon was made a national monument by President Theodore Roosevelt. Since then, the protected area has been expanded to 34,000 acres (13,760 hectares), and designated a national historical park. Chaco also has the honor of being one of just a few World Heritage Sites in all of North America.

Way out in New Mexico, in the heart of the American West, there is a haunted canyon. Chaco is its name.

Sunset gives the ruins a glowing beauty untouched by time.

To Find Out More

Here are some additional resources to help you learn more about Chaco Culture National Historic Park:

 **Books**

Lye, Keith. **Rocks and Minerals.** Raintree Steck-Vaughn, 1994.

McDonald, Mary A. **Rattlesnakes.** Children's Press, 1995.

Petersen, David. **Anasazi.** Children's Press, 1991.

Reed, Evelyn D. **Coyote Tales from the Indian Pueblos.** Sunstone Press, 1988.

Thompson, Kathleen. **New Mexico.** Raintree Steck-Vaughn, 1996.

Organizations and Online Sites

The Annenberg/CPB Project Exhibits Collection
http://www.learner.org/ exhibits/collapse/ chacocanyon.html

Look at archeological evidence to discover why the Chaco Canyon civilization fell. Try hands-on exhibits like "garbageology" and "Dating the Evidence."

Chaco Culture National Historical Park
P.O. Box 220
Nageezi, NM 87037-0220
http://www.nps.gov/chco

Great Outdoors Recreation Pages (GORP):Chaco Culture National Historical Park
http://www.gorp.com/gorp /resourse/us__nhp/nm__ chaco.htm

Information on hiking, camping, places to stay, wildlife, plant life, and more.

National Park Foundation
1101 17th Street N.W.
Suite 1008
Washington, DC 20036
http://www.nationalparks. org/guide/parks/ chaco-cultur-1857.htm

Practical visitor information—directions, activities, camping.

The National Park Service U.S. Dept. of the Interior
1849 C Street N.W.
Washington, DC 20240
http://www.nps.gov/chcu/

From this site you can visit the exhibit on Chaco Canyon at the Museum of Northern Arizona, and the Chaco Library and Photo Gallery. Check out nearby attractions such as Aztec Ruins National Monument and Mesa Verde National Monument.

Sipapu Chetro Ketl Great Kiva
http://sipapu.ucsb.edu/ html/kiva.html

Explore a three-dimensional reconstruction of a great kiva. An archeological description of the kiva is also featured.

Important Words

arid having little or no water

artifact personal possessions left behind by ancient cultures

artisan a craftsperson

ceremony a formal act, usually religious

culture a distinct group of people, often with a common language, race, and religion

excavate to uncover or unearth

fertile rich, able to grow or support life

irrigation a system of ditches and gates used to redirect the flow of water

mortar a mixture of sand and lime, used between stone or bricks

remote distant, or hard to reach